HEART-SHAPED LEAVES

Aphorisms, Adaptations, Improvisations and Essays

by

Shahin Khalilli

RB
Rossendale Books

Where your treasure is, there will your heart be also.

Matthew Arnold (1822-1888),
English poet and critic

Published by Lulu Enterprises Inc.
3101 Hillsborough Street
Suite 210
Raleigh, NC 27607-5436
United States of America

Published in paperback 2015
Copyright Shahin Khalilli © 2015
ISBN : 978-1-329-35191-2

CONTENTS

Acknowledgments

I would like to thank my respected colleagues, Fiala Abdullayeva and F. Alexander Magill for their invaluable suggestions on this project. I feel my thanks and gratitude to my editor as well.

In compiling the booklet titled as 'Heart-Shaped Leaves: Aphorisms, Adaptations, Improvisations and Essays' I thought much about Walt Whitman's stanzas:

O the joy of my spirit-it is uncaged –
It darts like lightening!

The same might be said of the compilation that the author is intending to deliver to his readers. I was eager to establish a close mixture of the ideas in poetry of some prominent writers whose work could sustain a comparison with some of my lighter poetic expressions.

The booklet is designed by the author to respond to the strong interest of readers about the realm of prosaic and poetical beauty.

Foreword

What I have in my mind and heart is sincere love and words of wisdom that make me cheerful and full of writing energy that I dare present them to my readers after 60 years on this earth.

Usually, distinguished poets and writers write the words of wisdom, but thinking that I also had my contribution to Azerbaijani Turkish Literature during the 40 years of my pedagogical and literary-scientific activity, as I also have the honor of a professorship, I dare say my thoughts about the British and American men of letters, along with my words of wisdom about life, made me compile them into this small book.

The title of the book 'Heart-Shaped Leaves' is not an arbitrary naming. One autumn day walking on the streets I gazed at the leaves falling down which reminded me of the years of my past life. I wanted to collect those yellow and reddish leaves and to stick them to the trees. But even the power of God wouldn't get them back to the trees. It's the power of God that gave them once the happiest days in Spring and Summer. Now it was time for me to think and write about my lost years that were like the pictures of the leaves in my life.

I am not a freelance poet or prose writer. It is true that my creation of rhymes especially for children has been published in Baku. And I have taught English for over forty years - I am a professor of English Literature at the Azerbaijan University of Languages. My monographic researches are on the theme of literary cultural connections with the English speaking world.

Finally, I would like to express my hope that the ideas in this book might provide my readers with many hours of enjoyment,

Shahin Khalilli
Baku, the Republic of Azerbaijan
January 2014

PART I

Quotes and Improvisations

❖ Alexander Pope wrote in his epigram intended for Sir Isaac Newton in Westminster-Abbey. How charming are the stanzas:

> *Nature and Nature's Laws lay hid in Night.*
> *God said,* **Let Newton be!** *and All was* **Light.**

We are intending our expression in the poetic style as the following:

> *The world's genius is Newton,*
> *Night is whitened in new tone.*

❖ Alfred Tennyson was a great Edwardian poet. In his 'Elaine's Song' we read:

> *Love, art thou sweet? then bitter death must be:*
> *Love, thou art bitter; sweet is death to me,*
> *O Love, if death be sweeter, let me die.*

'Elaine's Song' has a pessimistic tone but Elaine should be stronger than death. If you had heard about a Turkish heroine, like Tomiris, you had to be inspired by the great love of the two. My soul is singing with great love:

> *You had written the new song,*
> *Rise up, mister Tennyson!*
> *Who is leaning on the earth?*
> *Love is stronger than the death.*

❖ The poet John Clare in his poem 'Love Lives Beyond the Tomb' tried to present the poetic vision of love. What he thinks about love, is:

Love lives beyond
The tomb, the earth, the flowers, and dew,
I love the fond,
The faithful, young, and true.

Yet everybody is eager to find love, but it is invisible, which you will ever look for. My poetic concept about love is:

Love is nice as a rose
Love I love as a dove.
It's a poem, not a prose,
It is rhyming with above.

❖ Percy Bysshe Shelley:

Hope can borrow
From poor today, from rich tomorrow.

Me:

Hope is sweet as honey
But is chasing for love, and money.

❖ The disease called plague is known to the world as the 'Black Death'. The biographer Peter Ackroyd notes that '...*the plague came first to Venice, of all European cities. When a Venetian galley returned to its home port in the autumn of 1347, after a trading voyage to Caffa on the Black Sea, it carried within its hold certain black rats... The market of trade between East and West became the entrepot of death. Venice exported the epidemic, too... So the 'black death' of Europe began.*'

Me:

It's a historical fact that over three hundred years later the plague arrived in England as well and it was a big disaster not just for the British people but for most countries of the world.

So the moral of this brief story is that the 'Black Death' didn't have any mercy on tradersa or people who wanted to lead a long life.

❖ President Abraham Lincoln banned the slavery of blacks in 1863. Langston Hughes, the poet and the leader of the Harlem Renaissance, in his 'Dream Variations' produced the images of jazz music, expressing his heart soundings there as well:

Night coming tenderly
Black like me...

Me:

> *I do love when comes Night*
> *The Day is a new sight.*
> *Night like a Knight hugs the Day*
> *Tenderly and tight.*

❖ Sylvia Plath:

> *I am inhabited by a cry*
> *Nightly it flaps out*
> *Looking, with its hooks, for something to love.*

Me:

> *Your love was huge for Ted Hughes*
> *But it didn't last, - Miss Plath.*
> *Was it not love, or it became wrath,*
> *You took your love as a new path*
> *But, Alas! Why to die, Miss Plath.*

❖ The Osmanite, or Ottoman empire had a profound influence on English drama. The empire of the Turks
was a big danger at the gates of Western Europe. 55
out of 600 plays of the British Renaissance spoke
about the expansionist Osmanite empire and its
emperors.

Three British dramatists John Day, William Rowley, and George Wilkins dramatized their play 'The Travels of the Three English Brothers'. It describes the travel of brothers Thomas, Anthony and Robert Sherley to the Safavids empire. So the British audience could get a glimpse of the Safavids, or Azerbaijani Turkish emperor Shah Abbas, or the 'Sophy'. And it might be appreciated as the first literary dramatic acquaintance of British spectators with the Azerbaijani Turkish image. The play which had entered in the Stationers' Register in 1607 makes the establishment of British theatrical connection with Azerbaijan over 400 years. So the stage, or the performance of a play is not a lie, but truth of the vision in one area of the world with the brothers' eyes.

❖ William Butler Yeats wrote in his 'Song':
   O who could have foretold
   That the heart grows old?
Me:
   It's very smart you say he-art,
   But it isn't a cart, it's the heart.

❖ Percy Bysshe Shelley:

Thought

Alone, and its quick elements, Will,

Passion

Reason, Imagination, cannot die.

Me:

You ought

To live with thought, there is no

Other way,

Thought like the Moon is far

And away.

❖ William Shakespeare in his famous tragedy 'Macbeth'
wrote:

Life's but a walking shadow, a poor player

That struts and frets his hour upon the stage

And then is heard no more; it is a tale

Told by an idiot, full of sound and fury,

Signifying nothing.

Me:

We are all players on the stage of life

We are all pairs-thanks, we are all alive

We are strutting and fretting while we live

What is life? When we are getting old
We tightly hold the ground, but not the gold.

❖ William Shakespeare wrote this song in the epilogue of
'Twelfth Night' which says:

> *A great while ago the world begun,*
> *With a heigh! ho! the wind and the rain,*
> *But that's all one, our play is done,*
> *And we'll strive to please you every day.*

Me:

> *Leisure and pleasure has its measure,*
> *A man in the world is a great treasure.*
> *It is worth living ninety nine,*
> *With love, snow and Sunshine.*

❖ 'It was a Lover and his Lass'-that's title of the song,
sung by two pages in the play 'As You Like It!' by
William Shakespeare, where we read:

> *For love is crowned with the prime,*
> *In spring time, in spring time, in spring time,*
> *The only pretty ring time,*
> *When birds do sing,*
> *Hey ding a ding a ding,*
> *Hey ding a ding a ding,*
> *Hey ding a ding a ding,*
> *Sweet lovers love the spring.*

Me:

Love is Princess, I'm Prince
It's the season of the Spring.
Flowers-white and pink
Streams and springs are like an ink
They are rhyming,
I am miming
It's a warm ring
With a hey and ho in the Spring.

❖ Saul Bellow, a Jewish-American novelist awarded the Nobel Prize for Literature (1976) first was a Communist, but after World War II he became one of the prominent Existentialist writers. He was thinking that without God, or moral laws you are quite alone in a meaningless, or chaotic world. Why, and what to live for is the essential question for a man. A search for the meaning of life is like a question of 'To be, or not to be'. The Jewish mind and Jewish experience proved Jewish existence.

❖ The most joyful American poet E. E. Cummings always wrote his name as 'e.e. cummings' so as to be distinguished from other writers. He usually didn't capitalize words, but sometimes he used capital letters in the mid or the end of some words. But he hated

Politics, the Church, Big Business, and the coldness of Science. So as a poet he was strange, but he couldn't win the competition of poets to be the first. He was never praised or cursed in the study of modern literature.

❖ William Davies:

Sing out, my Soul, thy songs of joy;
  Such as a happy bird will sing
Beneath a Rainbow's lovely arch
  In early spring.

Me:

Soul is dancing, but not feet,
  As though it is sailing with the fleet.
And the Rainbow makes a bow,
  How great is the Carnival. Vow!

❖ F. Scott Fitzgerald who just lived for forty four years created his marvelous novel 'The Great Gatsby' in which the hero Gatsby believes that money could buy love and happiness. But the hero sees his tragic fate. And the writer was also descended of rich parents and married to Zelda and had a daughter Scottie. His wife's mental illness made him lead the tragic fate like his hero.

❖ When I attended the XXV British Writing Conference in 1999, one of British writers talking to me said that I looked very much like Samuel Beckett. I was surprised because I had never seen his photograph up to that time. And I asked the very young visiting Irish lady writer to assist me finding Beckett's photo. She told me what I still remember:

–*Why the photo, you are alive Beckett...*

Fourteen years later I heard the same words from one of my students. That time my answer was:

–You are right, his surname is Beckett, and I'm Bakuvite. As for origin, we are countrymen. His Homeland was Irene (Ireland), mine not Iran, but Arran (nowadays Azerbaijan).

❖ In one of the Limericks we read:

There was a Young Man of Typhoo
Who wanted to catch the 2.02,
Said the trainman: 'Don't hurry,
Or worry, or flurry-
It's minute or two to 2.02!'

Me:

There were two men of Shaki
One wanted to sit in front, the other in back
Said the driver: 'Why argue
The taxi will take you
With its front and back to Baku'.

❖ Benjamin Franklin noted that:

When men and women die, as poets sung, his heart's the last part moves, her last, the tongue.

But we think:

When stone-hearted men and women die, no parts of their body shake. You might say it's wrong, they die suddenly.

❖ This is an English nursery rhyme:

Solomon Grundy
Born on Monday,
Christened on Tuesday,
Married on Wednesday,
Took ill on Thursday,
Worse on Friday,
Died on Saturday,
Buried on Sunday,
This is the end
Of Solomon Grundy.

Me:

The Moon was the first —
Gave its name to Monday
God of Darkness —
Tuesco became Tuesday.
Woden-God of War
Started game on Wednesday.
God of Thor-the Thunderer
Had a flame on Thursday.
Goddess Freia walked
Like a dame on Friday.
God of Saturn talked
Like a lame on Saturday.
God of Sun blushed in red
Was last in shame on Sunday.

❖ If Romanticism is the son of Enlightenment, Renaissance is its stepfather.

❖ Samuel Taylor Coleridge was first designated as 'the founder of the romantic school of poetry'. And if he didn't write romances there wouldn't be echoes of poetic news.

❖ Percy Bysshe Shelley wrote in his essay 'A Defence of Poetry' :

Poets are the unacknowledged legislators of the world.

Me:

Parliament is itself a great poet of the time.

❖ Romanticism is not the world of dreams, but cries or screams for the better life of people's streams.

❖ John Keats wrote when he was 22 years old:

I think I shall be among the English Poets after my death.

Me:

Life after death reminds me Ovid's 'Metamorphoses'.

❖ Was Shakespeare a plagiarist? No, he was a playwright. Hamlet made a risk, showed his wrist, who didn't believe it.

❖ James Joyce wrote after print of his famous 'Ulysses': For myself, I always write about Dublin, because if I can get to the heart of Dublin I can get to the heart of all cities of the world.

Me:

June 16 1904, just one day in which the major action of the 'Ulysses' is set, all in Homer's 'Odyssey' was removed in, and the Homerian world was exchanged with Dublin life. So Homer became a modern James Joyce in Dublin. Homer was doubled with Dublin.

❖ The literary world of Orthodox on the whole copied out Greek, and Roman literature and literary genres, and the Orient had a similar way, most Muslim literature is based upon Persian, and Arabian literary genres as well. And if you tie these two literatures together, world literature will be unique.

❖ Fame and good name live on after men's death. O, God bless you. Never miss to do your best in this flying Earth.

❖ 'Gilgamesh' of ancient Sumeria is not a series of games written on 12 clay tablets, but it is an ancient story of the world. And if you want to know more about immortality, never try to get more, as death was given by God to be a man's share.

❖ John Ruskin:

All books are divisible into two classes: the books of the hour, and the books of all time.

Me:

It is not polite to gaze at somebody's eyes. Eyes are not books to read. Better read hearts that are not so easy as you think.

❖ William Shakespeare:

Love looks not with the eyes, but with the mind.

Me:

It's a good saying: Love is blind. But beautiful love is not on the seventh hills of the sky; you can find it, if you talk to the heart, or mind.

❖ Socrates:

As for me, all I know is that I know nothing.

Me:

Nothing is a great thing. All philosophers wrote everything, that's why they turned to nothing.

❖ Benjamin Franklin:

Early to bed and early to rise,

Makes a man healthy, wealthy and wise.

Me:

Better have a good sleep at night, might, or wisdom may be late, never mind.

❖ The first newspaper in the world, the *Gazetta* was established in Venice at the beginning of the XVII century.

Scandals, quarrels, gossips were the fuel of the city, but the waters around Venice didn't allow the city to be engulfed in flames.

❖ George Gordon Byron was amazed with the passionate kisses of the women of Venice:

The women kiss better than those of any other nation.

Me:

Kissing has became a disastrous tradition among men now. If you were alive, Mr. Byron, in the Caucasus you might have the best enjoyment.

❖ Mr. Edgar Allan Poe first tried his talent in a poetry, so he was a great poet. But Poe's popularity in prose was much more great, so he became the founder of the detective genre, and science fiction in America. But

Poe was a poet as well, there was a need just to add the letter 't' to his famous surname.

❖ Robert Burns in Scotland, and Robert Frost in the USA were not much worried about the weather. The former had the sun, or fire in his heart, and the second poet wasn't much afraid of cold, and frost, because his second name was Frost.

❖ Mr. Truman had the right to be President of the USA, and if he had had the surname of Falseman, everybody might have crossed his name not wanting him to be elected to the highest post.

❖ James Joyce has a very good-sounding name. I knew a lady scholar who defended her thesis about Joyce's creativity. Some three years later she forgot the writer's name saying what exactly was his name?

❖ James Joyce in his 'Ulysses' played mythic correspondences mostly by eliminating the titles of chapters which he had chosen from Homer. So James Joyce might be the best plagiarist of Homer.

❖ Gabriel Garcia Marquez, a Colombian writer wouldn't be famous with his 'One Hundred Years of Solitude' and received the Nobel Prize for Literature if he hadn't sold his car, so that his family couldn't bother him much and live on the money from the sale of the car.

❖ Vladimir Nabokov, Russian-born American novelist was known as the king of contemporary fiction. He was not a true king, but a fiction king.

❖ 'Being and Nothingness' resulted in Jean-Paul Sartre being awarded the Nobel Prize in 1964. So one can be very prominent with such a formula.

❖ Virginia Woolf's husband Leonard was Jewish and was captured by the Nazis, and their London apartment was destroyed. This resulted in the writer drowning in the River Ouse, but her fame is still great as with her first novel 'The Voyage Out'.

❖ It is a great success of our modern times to live with the 'stream of consciousness'. But postmodernist writers will be taken into an asylum one day.

❖ Franz Kafka who was the son of a rich Jewish family had the writer's fame only after his death. He became known as a prominent figure of German culture and literature. If he hadn't worked in an insurance office his fame wouldn't be so great.

❖ John Keats:

'Beauty is truth, truth beauty', - that is all
Ye know on earth, and all ye need to know.

Me:

Beauty is beauty, and truth is truth —
Why should lie it? Check it through.

❖ John Heywood:

Better unborn than untaught.

Me:

Every speaker is not a teacher. A good teacher makes a man from iron.

❖ Henry Clay:

I had rather be right, than be President.

Me:

My message is sent: the right man never becomes President.

❖ George Henry Borrow:
Translation is at best an echo.

Me:
Better have one language, not two.

❖ Charles Dickens:
Regrets are the natural property of grey hairs.

Me:
Grey hairs are the symbol of hard life and its affairs.

❖ Ralph Waldo Emerson:
The first wealth is health.

Me:
The second wealth is a purse full of money.

❖ Jerome Klapka Jerome:
We drink one another's health and spoil our own.

Me:
Before drinking wine we say:
—Cheers!
Before drinking to someone's health, we should say:
—Tears!

❖ Mark Twain (Samuel Langhorne Clemens):
Man is the only animal that blushes. Or needs to.

Me:
Any man should know that it is not a lie, there is the hidden 'man' in the 'animal': one is tall, the other is small.

❖ Henry David Thoreau:
Read the best books first, or you may not have a chance to read them at all.

Me:
Best books are very rare, if you read worst ones you will never know which is the best.

❖ Percy Bysshe Shelley:
Our sweetest songs are those that tell of saddest thought.

Me:
The song expressing sorrow is always smart and it brings the light into the heart.

❖ George Bernard Shaw:

We don't bother much about dress and manners in England because as a nation we don't dress well and we've no manners.

Me:

If no good dress and manners then let banners speak.

❖ William Shakespeare:

A good heart's worth gold.

Me:

If you have a good head, go ahead.

❖ William Shakespeare:

Men of few words are the best men.

Me:

Men without words are great.

❖ William Shakespeare:

The fool doth think he is wise, but the wise knows to be a fool.

Me:

If the fool and wise can't arrange their places, then they are both fools.

❖ Thomas Paine:

The world is my country, all mankind are my brethren, and to do good is my religion.

Me:

Mr. Paine, you were a man of the 18th century, perhaps you led the very good life, you didn't have any sorrow and pain. Why didn't you change your surname to Mr. Joy?

❖ Henry David Thoreau:

Every man is the builder of a temple, called his body.

Me:

If men had to wear skirts, that temple might look very strange. Better call women the best architect, who take much better care of their bodies.

❖ William Makepeace Thackeray:

A good laugh is sunshine in a house.

Me:

But a smile is moonlight at night.

❖ Alfred Tennyson:

'Tis better to have loved and lost
Than never to have loved at all.

Me:

The man is born with love -
Within embracement in dance
He never dies, some after death
Live in Louvre, in France.

❖ Robert Louis Stevenson:

The cruellest lies are often told in silence.

Me:

The lies never fly like a sound, but they crawl like snakes on the ground.

❖ Mark Twain (Samuel Langhorne Clemens):

In Boston they ask, How much does he know? In New York, How much is he worth? In Philadelphia, Who were his parents?

Me:

Mr. Clemens! In Azerbaijan they ask, Who is his uncle?

❖ William Shakespeare wrote:

All the World's a stage,
And all the men and women merely players.

My response:

In this case you needn't rebuilt the new theatre,
like 'the Globe'.

❖ Heinrich Heine:
The Romans would never have had time to conquer the world if
they had been obliged to learn Latin first of all.

We:
The Romans conquered the world with the power of Latin
alphabet; if they didn't have the ABC, English might not have
explored the world and the word.

❖ Mr. William Wordsworth, not just your surname, but
your words are worth reading.

❖ George Gordon Byron wrote:
He who loves not his country, can love nothing.

When I read Byron's statement, I hesitated and could
whisper the following:
Why did you write it, Mr. Byron, it's wrong. You never loved
your country; one can try telling that your truth seems to the
clients as a sparkling menu.

❖ Lewis Carrol:

Take care of the sense, and the sounds will take care of themselves.

Me:

Take care of the tense, and the teacher of Grammar will check your sense.

❖ George Eliot (Mary Ann Evans):

No man can be wise on an empty stomach.

Me:

An empty head never heard how to go ahead.

❖ O. Henry (William Sydney Porter):

Love and business and family and religion and art and patriotism are nothing but shadows of words when a man's starving.

Me:

When a man is rich and wealthy he sees the world like a small ball.

❖ Vladimir Ilyich Lenin (Ulyanov), the founder of the socialist system wrote in his report 'The Tasks of the Youth Leagues':

You can become a Communist only when you enrich your mind with the knowledge of all treasures created by mankind.

Me:

To be a Communist is like a summer mist; make a risk, you will eat just a crisp.

❖ Henry Wadsworth Longfellow:

Music is the universal language of mankind.

But I think:

Birds are the universal creatures of the world, wherever they fly, they sing the same understandable song.

❖ William Somerset Maugham:

People ask you for criticism, but they only want praise.

But I claim:

Ladies like roses and presents; and praise is enjoyment and delight.

❖ John Milton:

The childhood shows the man,
As morning shows the day.

Me:

The water leads the way to the sea.
And roughness is running after mercy.

❖ Marcus Aurelius Antoninus:

My city and country, so far as I am Antoninus, is Rome, but so
far as I am a man, it is the World.

Me:

The glory of one nation, or of its emperor is not eternal. Neither
fraternal, no maternal empire can live for one millennium.

❖ Emily Dickinson wrote the following stanzas about
the fame:

Fame is a bee
It has a song –
It has a sting –
Ah, too, it has a wing.

What we think when we don't have the fame:

Fame is a name
Walks like a dame.
Fame is courage,
But not a shame.

❖ The English poet Wyatt was telling:
> *My most desire my hand may reach:*
> *My will is always at my hand.*

But I think:
> *Why you should be the slave of your will,*
> *The game is over, your lover is nil.*

❖ The other poet of England, Surrey presented a complaint by night of the lover not beloved:
> *Bringing before my face the great increase*
> *Of my desires, whereat I weep and sing.*
> *In joy and woe, as in a doubtful ease,*
> *For my sweet thoughts sometime do pleasure bring.*

My feeling in rhyming is:
> *I think joy and woe like day and night*
> *Is the whole life pleasure and delight.*

❖ The poet Sidney who Elizabeth I loved and evaluated greatly, wrote:
> *Leave me o love, which reachest but to dust,*
> *And thou my mind aspire to higher things:*
> *Grow rich in that which never taketh rust:*
> *What ever fades, but fading pleasure brings.*

The poetry is great when it is bright, and what response is:

Love is not an iron, which can take rust,
Divine love is greatest, in love I trust.

❖ Edmund Spenser wrote in his 'Fairy Queen':

In springing flower the image of thy day;
Ah see the Virgin Rose, how sweetly she.

The poet Spenser was also a good scholar. When he finished writing his treatise 'A View of the Present State of Ireland' he tried to present his historical accounts of Scythian tribes fleeing from the shores of the Caspian Sea into modern areas of Scotland and Ireland. So we get the ancient news how Albyne Scythians gave their names to Scotland, and Irene, or Arran Scythians founded the second Scythia as Ireland (or Arranland, but not Iran Land as Thomas Moore noted).

My response is:

The fairest, the best, the Virgin Elizabeth,
Married to England, from her birth.

❖ James Joyce wrote in one of his primarily descriptive poems that:

The grey winds, the cold winds are blowing
Where I go.
I hear the noise of many waters
Far below,
All day, all night, I hear them flowing
To and fro.

The major attraction of this poem made me express the following:

All day you heard the nature's voice
That's rejoice.
The wind's and the water's noise
Is great Mr. Joyce
Now your deathbed is near the Zoo
The Lions roaring –
You made the choice.

❖ Robert Burns was 37 years old when he died of rheumatic fever. But his verses will live forever, his great contributions to the British poetry, the poems in the style of old ballads will bring him everlasting fame, as a songwriter the best and the first. The song 'For the Sake o' Somebody' is one of the songs of Burns' love passion. We read the following:

I would wake a winter night
For the sake o' Somebody.
    O-hon! For Somebody!
    O-hey! For Somebody!
I could range the world around
For the sake o' Somebody.

The common use of poetic style and language, and the spirit of the real ploughman poet has the magnetism which makes you think about the power of love.

But we think:

Love is waiting for the night
When is burning candle light
    O-no! Mr. Burns
    O-ney! Mr. Burns.
You are brave-that is why,
But I know, love is shy.

❖ Robert Frost:
A bank is a place where they lend you an umbrella in fair weather and ask for it back when it begins to rain.

Me:

A Money bank is not a river bank. But you might indeed become wet if you don't have an umbrella on a bank.

❖ Benjamin Franklin:
   Early to bed and early to rise,
   Makes a man healthy, wealthy and wise.

Me:
   Early love and early marriage
   Indeed is a big carriage.

❖ Anton Pavlovich Chekhov:
   If I hadn't been a writer, I think I should have been a gardener.

Me:
   Earth is worthless without the word, so the word like the Sun is circling all around the world.

❖ Sir James Matthew Barrie:
   Poets are people who despise money except what you need for today.

Me:
   Bees have a small portion of honey for their only use per day, so bees are like poets indeed.

❖ George Gordon Byron:

Truth is always strange, -
Stranger than fiction.

Me:

Fiction is ignoring, -
Truth is uproaring.

❖ *No Homer, No Greece*
No Hugo, No Paris.

❖ The Venetian proverb says:

Money is our second blood.

Me:

Blood is running in the veins to catch the money in the brain.

❖ William Blake addressed his readers:

To see a World in a Grain of Sand,
And a Heaven in a Wild Flower:
Hold Infinity in the palm of your hand,
And Eternity in an hour.

Me:

A World of Words is pure and sweet

A Heaven is tuning its music above.
Infinity is hidden like the wind
    Eternity is life after death, or love.

❖ J.B. O'Reilly:

    The red rose whispers of passion,
        And the white rose breathes of love;
    O, the red rose is a falcon,
        And the white rose is a dove.

Me:

    The black rose with its delight,
        Is singing a song of the Earth;
    But in the light of the night,
        It is like a black crow, or the Death.

❖ William Shakespeare wrote in his 'The Merchant of Venice':

The Moon shines bright. In such a night as this. When the sweet wind did gently kiss the trees and they did make no noise, in such a night…

Me:

    How beautiful is the night
        The Moon shines calm and bright.
    Trees are standing as an actress
        Wind is eager for the kiss.

❖ William Shakespeare in 'Hamlet-the Prince of Denmark':

Words without thoughts never to heaven go.

Me:

Pure spirits are usually intending to find a homage on the heaven.

❖ William Shakespeare in 'Hamlet-the Prince of Denmark':

If we are true to ourselves, we can not be false to anyone.

Me:

If truth is everywhere, who we will be fighting against the evil then.

❖ R. L. Stevenson wrote:

Bright is the ring of words
When the right man rings them,
Fair the fall of songs
When the singer sings them.

Me:

You are right, words are bright
Words are ringing in the tune.
Love is dancing every night
If the Moon has the light.

❖ The English Biographer Peter Ackroyd writes in his newly printed book 'Venice. Pure City':

'There are in fact borrowings and adaptations - of Islamic architecture and Islamic art-throughout the city. Even the Venetian colors, ultramarine blue and gold, are derived from the Middle East. The trade routes, the organized seagoing caravans, even the craft guilds, of Venice were Muslim in origin... In the paintings of Carpaccio, for example, Venetian interiors are shown to be decorated with objects of eastern provenance; the throne of the Virgin in Gentile Bellini's 'Virgin and Child Enthroned' is placed carefully on a Turkish carpet or prayer rug.'

Me:

Is Venice the second Constantinople, or not? If there is something oriental mixed with orthodox it means that not just a city, but the world itself is worth living, and dying.

❖ Peter Ackroyd:

'There are forty references by Shakespeare to Venice ... Two of his plays, The Merchant of Venice (1598) and Othello (1602) are set wholly or partly in that city... It has been proposed by some scholars that Shakespeare actually visited the city, but that is most unlikely. He did not need to do so. Venice is pre-eminently an imagined city.'

Me:

Venice emerging as a trade centre in the fourth century was the plot of Shakespeare's two plays because in London during the reign of Elizabeth I there was a keen interest in Jews who were expelled from England as the physician of the queen was intending to poison her, and Arabians, or Turks were a great danger to the English in Elizabethan times, and they mostly had a good power and trade in Venice. Shakespeare had a power and talent not just of shaking the scene in London, but all around the world.

❖ Robert Hayman wrote in his epigram 'A Mad Answer of a Madman' the following lines:
One asked a madman if a wife he had.
'A wife?' quoth he. 'I never was so mad'.

Me:

I would tell you otherwise,
Madman speaking very wise.

❖ The following two lines for a Christmas card by Hilaire Belloc sounds like that:
May all my enemies go to hell,
Noel, Noel, Noel, Noel.

If I were offered to write a poetical sketch for a Christmas card I would utter these stanzas:

Why to shout, why to yell
Enemies will go to hell.
There is no other way,
Let them leave far away.
No yell, no yell, no yell, no yell,
Noel, Noel, Noel, Noel.

PART II

The Literary Scenes, or Multifaceted Pictures

of Modern Life

❖ In the fall time you can see lots of leaves lying on the ground. It seemed to me that some of the leaves were in the shape of a heart or the fingers of the hand. As though trees announced their love to the soil, and threw out their hearts on it as the symbol of their great desire to join their partner-lover. So the trees cut their hands off and threw them on the soil, saying that they were quite naked, as they were going nearly to die, if the soil would reject the big love of the trees.

❖ Your love drives me mad, - what will I do with my car 'Mazda', I have my driving license.

❖ A grave is a good place for a man to relax, your wife will not be much worried about the salary, and a tax.

❖ In the realm of beauty you have to know your duty: they say there are seven beauties, you must choose one, but not two.

❖ Never sigh if your age is plenty. There is no use to say—

   I am fifty.
   But you can say —I'm two 25.

❖ What do the words - a man and woman mean?

Man-Me admire nude
Woman-We own man.

❖ If human history begins about two million years ago in Africa, the earliest 'humanlike' species four hundred thousand years later began migrating out of Africa. And after another million and a quarter years they spread to the areas of the Eastern Hemisphere. What they learned first; how and when to use the fire and the development of speech for communication. Agriculture had changed their physical appearance greatly. So agriculture led the people to civilization, and they say that Western civilizations emerged in Mesopotamia about 3200 BC.

❖ Who am I? That is not the question of ancient times, and of the prehistoric world. So the search for the self is like the search for hell.

❖ If light is born out of darkness, the night accuses light for being so naughty, but not very polite.

❖ We usually have had red roses, but in Holland they grow black ones. In the Heavens we usually see red stars and if somebody is intending to paint stars with the colour of night…

O my God! The stars might collapse like the starry USSR.

- ❖ The eyes of all peoples are upon the peace - it is a masterpiece of all creations and nations.

- ❖ If you perceive a laugh, you will receive a love.

- ❖ The word is a king; even when the war starts and finishes, the word becomes the first and the last.

- ❖ If you have just four pence,
  I don't think you might have a normal sense.

- ❖ Love and melody are like a man and a lady who are singing an eternal hymn of the world.

- ❖ A child's dream is like the stream that is eager to find itself in the sea.

- ❖ An ape was in a good shape, but it didn't like a school in the forest, it wanted to join the students of a humanitarian school.

- ❖ University and a city, they are like twins. But a village was intending for construction of the higher education as Uni-village.

❖ The world is very generous: it gives us what it has. But sometimes it blushes with revenge against the people, and its sharp arm is an earthquake.

❖ Pictorial writing was the first book for beginners. Now people prefer air writing in the modern age, that is air language.

❖ Bakuvites are residents of the capital city of Azerbaijan. So they wake up and go to bed with the wind on most days. And one can say that wind and wife are reliable friends to man to the end of his life.

❖ Snow turns into red when there is no pomegranate in winter.

❖ People pretend to be polite, though they are wild by nature. So changing the image of wilderness most people are practicing to be vegetarians.

❖ We play with a monkey, thinking that it has a very good instinct for better understanding the human gestures and languages. One is a man, and the other is mon. But the second syllable in the word monkey is the key. A man usually has a key in his pocket, but the monkey doesn't keep it in secret when it is on the tree.

❖ Better say 'Hi', not 'How do you do!' Someone might say 'Mind your own business. I know how to do things.'

❖ The Sky is like a whiteboard; it is for the God who writes the destiny of people who hoard.

❖ Love is in the heart, it is a great art.

❖ The old tribe of Angles behaved like angels.

❖ England means the land of Angles and Saxons, so there was no need to make the long sounding, and at the end they coined the conjunction 'and'.

❖ Love and laugh were very happy together: Love embraced laugh as its better-half.

❖ The number of words reminds us the number of leaves on trees: winds talk to leaves when summer leaves, but people use much words when there is nowhere to go, and nothing to do.

❖ If someone is taught, he can gain a thought.

❖ The forest is a good chamber for most animals. And most men find it the best place for a rest.

❖ Earth is a good place for birth, love and death.

❖ Western scholars say that men have about sixty thousand thoughts a day; but we consider that we have a thousand and one thoughts a day. Better have less thoughts, but more oughts.

❖ The founder of America is Spanish, the speakers are English, what you say is OK, - USA is not UK.

❖ Money is like the Moon, it disappears in the day time.

❖ Man who doesn't fear God, one day will play soccer with a hippopotamus.

❖ Honey makes good money.

❖ Pronouns had a quarrel with nouns - we announce that you are under our dominion.

❖ A diplomat is the only man who never thinks that he has got a diploma.

❖ If trees had two legs, they wouldn't hug the soil.

❖ The Roman emperors: Augustus's name became the 8th month of the year - as August, but Julius Caesar's name was given to the 7th month - July.

❖ The Universe is good rhyming with a verse, so it is on the whole a unique verse that we adore.

❖ Love is as white as a dove, and it flies in the sky not as a dove, but like an arrow, it is not a joy, but sorrow.

❖ There is a very good name for the flower - 'forget me not'; how could I forget you, you remind me my first love, which was my first magnet.

❖ A madman is not a bad man. He tells what he sees.

❖ A madman never walks in the mud - he says that he is not an ass, better walk on the grass.

❖ If marriage is madness, then solitude through all your life is grief and sadness.

❖ Marriage is like the carriage of an age.

❖ Love is blind - never mind, if love finds you, it will waste your pockets like gold coins.

❖ The father, mother and the son were in the car. Suddenly the son says:
  –Father, look at the bird.
  The mother was surprised, she couldn't see any bird. Just the father and the son could see it - the bird was a lady walking on the street.

❖ Love is like a stove. If you fell into it, you have to strive to the end of your life.

❖ Silence is not golden, but a great science.

❖ Venice (the word originates from *Venuce* the goddess that was born from the sea and ice) as a city was built upon water. The city is famous for its pigeons as well. And Venice became the very first centre of opera throughout Europe. If you see the woman on the balcony it reminds you of a familiar Venetian motif as though they were imprisoned at home. But it is a way for sexual display. So Venice itself was portrayed as the symbol of the beloved woman as well. (Peter Ackroyd)

Me:
> Venice is very nice on water and ice.

❖ A bribe makes the worst to stand on the right hand of the best.

❖ A lady from the mountains was very slim and tender - it seemed to me she was a fountain alive.

❖ The first poet of England named Caedmon was a shepherd; William Shakespeare with a beard became a bard of English, but he looked like a pork-butcher. Elizabeth I - 'lion-hearted lady' was the sinister Queen of England; and 'an Iron lady' Margaret Thatcher born on the thatcher of the shop had twin children and became a prime minister.

❖ If the chickens were not hens and cocks, they would follow watches or clocks and first would read the amusing books of Charles Dickens.

- It is said - that is a big surprise - if Nobel were noble he would not deliver a prize.

- No bell was not for Nobel, it's just he called himself Noble, preceding one letter made him to have the great name.

- Bees make honey, we make money.

- In the postmodern era you are much thinking, we are sure one day you might be really not a tall, but a thin king.

- Walter Scott had the surname of Scots origin and he carried his name all his life, to his great admiration and hesitation the name of his novel 'Ivanhoe' was given to the station.

- What do you want? - Just a wife. What is wrong? - You are right - it is life.

- What is best? -Work and rest.

- Who is your wife? - One is Daylight, the other is Night.

- If you tell me who you are, I will tell you who I am not.

- In the times of Druidism the people worshipped the Sun, the Moon and the Serpent. Now the Sun, the Moon and the Serpent worship men because they live in the postmodern era, not in ancient times.

- When one of my students writes a word she omits a letter at the beginning, when the second one writes a word she does it in the middle, but when I write I do that error at the end. If it comes from the stream of consciousness there is no use crying over mis-use.

- A man is dying - it is a continuous process. But if a man falls in love - it is very short or sudden - you will forget it forever.

- There are two loves: one is red, the other is white. Red love is like a red wine, but white one is divine love - it is love of God.

- To bear, or not to bear, if a guest is a bear, a fear will lie under the chair.

- Once I was talking to my students about flowers, of which for me the best of all was forget-me-not. A lady student was very interested in the flower that I was talking about. She asked me where it was growing.

– On the head, - was my answer. And she blushed in red for asking such a foolish question.

❖ Who is gentle, who is brute? - The emperor's name was Brute, who gave his name to the country Briton. So Brute of Troy spoke a broken Greek and preached to be a Graeco-British nation from the pre-historic, ancient epoch.

❖ Love has the dual face and grade. The first is bachelor, but the second is marriage.

❖ Green tea is not the guarantee of your life - just the wife which might send you either to hell, or paradise.

❖ The world is a big, big market, but there are many manholes in it, you can buy everything here, but if you want to see the souls watch your steps, you can fall into holes.

❖ When you are smoking a pipe, do you think that you are the king of smoke, or just a pauper of the choke…

❖ I still remember when I was five, and one day I attended the wedding party for the first time in my life. It is a national tradition that the ladies throw various sweets and small pieces of bread upon the bride's head when she enters the threshold of bridegroom's apartment, and children gather sweets fallen on the ground. Unfortunately I could get none and cried a lot. Seeing that, some ladies calmed me down and gave me lots of sweets. But I didn't stop crying, so the ladies wanted to know the reason. My answer was that I wanted not the sweets but the bride herself. Since that time I have been just thinking about the sweets, and about the brides who seem to me much more sweeter than everything in the world.

❖ Albanians have been much known to everybody - ancient Britain, Caucasian Albania, European Albania. Who were the first Albanians, nobody knows. But we know one thing: it has one meaning as the 'white land': Albion in England; Alba for Scotland. In the Celtic language it has the same meaning. Possibly it meant snow-covered mountains like in the Caucasus. Modern Azerbaijani Turks in the Caucasus in 4th to 6th centuries were called Albanians, and the country was called Albania.

❖ Most Americans call themselves Caucasians. Originally the races inhabited in the Caucasus were called the Caucasians. So we are twins.

❖ One-lettered word 'I' is not just a letter, but a unique word not of the alphabet, but of the world.

❖ If you think you are wise, read no more, you can be foolish otherwise.

❖ The ponds wrote an appeal to God which said that because of weakness of the rain they could not become the lakes.

❖ The animals were planning to establish a postmodern high school in the forest, but it didn't work, because the bear cannot bear the schooling in the cold winter time when he is in a deep sleep.

❖ The suffix 'an' at the end of the surnames is specific for Irishmen, 'son' for English, and 'Mac' is just prefix of the surnames for Scots. The real British might make the blend of the triad, saying that I am Macsonan - as their original surname.

❖ John is for an English, Sean is for an Irish, Mac is for a Scottish - nobody pities for their national identity.

❖ When you are reading a book of fiction you smile, or laugh you might consider that you lead two lives: one is borrowed, another is joy and sorrow.

❖ If humor is not a gossip or rumor, how is it going with people on tour for one or two hours a day.

❖ Reading four words of wisdom is worth visiting the four countries of the United Kingdom.

❖ London is like a thunder for those who haven't seen it. But when you visit the capital city, you imagine that you have the diploma of Earthquake University.

❖ *One, two, three-*
One is ocean
Two is wooden
Where is three —
It is hidden
Under tree

❖ *Who is grieving?*
  Words alone.
  Where is poet
  Butler Yeats.
  He could lead us
  To saloon.

❖ Romantics in England had not just the influence of ancient Roman culture and literature, but it never forgot the tremendous cultural heritage of the Romans. So how could the romantics forget about their relatives and real men? In short, there are 2 Roman periods in Britain: 1st is from 55 BC to 400 AD, 2nd is from 1780 to 1830.

❖ What is the 1st: an egg or chicken?
  Who is the 1st: a man or woman?
  If a man weren't the first how could a woman bore a child? That's a great puzzle. If there weren't the 1st lady who brought the man to the world? Then you might say: They both were sent from the Heaven as a gift of God.

❖ If the man weren't given the name, it's true, but not a fun, in the history of naming the fame alone could be an orphan.

❖ The world is the best, when the Sun is walking upon its breast.

❖ In the former Soviet times people started reading and writing, and doing everything in its limits, but never had the progress summits.

❖ Beowulf means a bee and a wolf, or a bear and a wolf, and some say that he was the bright, or a wise wolf. Do you know any other wolf who had been playing the English golf…

❖ The window is for the wind, the ending 'ow', means that it is on the wall.

❖ Door - means do, or; there is an alternative - or break. But the door is for women, windows are for men.

❖ A couple of dews on the grasses were in the orchard like sunglasses.

❖ Otherwise O would advise: never bother your friend, let wise be the first, and others the second.

❖ Onion is a union of the slightest dominions on the hell, thus it makes somebody weeping if they are not going on well.

❖ With the psycho-geographical investigation of history we become wiser, due to the talent and generosity of the man we discover not the city, but its writer.

❖ *I am singing*
Who am I?
I am thinking –
Butterfly.

It is better
Just to fly.
It is true
Not a lie.

You are tender,
You are light.
One day life –
One day flight.

❖ The world's common language is love. When the devil appears, it becomes a coward.

❖ In ancient times poetry was written and recited for an aristocratic audience: seeing the poor people without wisdom the writers pitied them so they transferred words into simple prose so they could understand it.

❖ Fever is not forever, but endeavor is always made in favor of winning the goal.

❖ Treason is a tragedy of one act. So the prison is built for that reason. It is a tact.

❖ Pleasure is nice at leisure time, it is a secret treasure of life.

❖ The city of Baku in Azerbaijan was built from oil, gas, and wind. The last word, wind, was given as a nickname to the city - that means a 'windy city' like Chicago.

❖ I met a lady in a class, she was of an older age, but she learned to count from one to six. She finished counting with six, and mispronounced it like 'sex'. It was her dream in learning the social language.

❖ In the Medieval Period the handwriting or manuscripts were not in copies, book printing by Caxton in about the 1470s destroyed the handwriting method, and it gave rise completely to book printing. Now internet books are competing with book printing. Who will win, nobody has come to the right decision yet?

❖ Asia or East, people are fond of leisure and feast. But what will Europe, or Orthodox do, when Asia or East will not play on a rope.

❖ The word 'drama' is originated from the Greek word 'dram' that means 'to do' or 'to act'. And the name 'tragedy' was applied to drama, also from Greek word 'tragos', means 'goat'. So one might say the tragic drama is not bulls', but goats' dueling.

❖ Theatre appeared in England in the 1560s, when Shakespeare wasn't born. So it wasn't Shakespeare who brought the theatre onto its stage, but the theatre took the hands of Shakespeare to the outdoors.

❖ The Globe Theatre as a stage was second in England, when the Globe, or the world that we live in was the big stage. Shakespeare wrote that the Globe Theatre was round or octagonal. So Shakespeare recreated the mini round theatre on the vast world theatre, wasn't it a plagiarism then?

❖ Women in Elizabethan Times didn't perform on the stage of Globe Theatre, instead men and boys acted in the roles of women. But Elizabeth I was not a man acting as the Queen, she was a lion-hearted lady.

❖ While thinking about the American idea, it makes you say: Oh, my God! Oh, my Dear! Where is the Prince, and the Princess? And it makes you think about the life, liberty and the pursuit of happiness. If we can't get into Trinity, we eat pineapples like monkeys.

❖ The plaice has one face:
The men, the Moon and the Sun has two.

❖ If no sense, nonsense will sneeze.

❖ In some cities of the world the drivers park their cars on the pavements. The pedestrians are intending to write an appeal to a mayor of a city to tie a rope on trees so they could pass on their way to their destination. And it will be good for their health, and our pedestrians might be genuine rope-walkers then.

❖ The black crows are crowned while in winter it snows.

❖ One day the king of the animals the Lion talked to his counterparts that from today on, all the animals have to speak the Lionese language so they could have the mutual understanding among them. The rabbit couldn't utter the roaring of the lion and was still thinking about its close neighbors like the fox and wolf, they might not be so dangerous after the new language will be in use by everybody.

❖ The eggs of the hens are taken for a sale into the market. The cocks appealed to the court that it was not fair as the householders do not regard them, they should be taken into prison. But the householders accused the cocks of wasting time - not even giving one egg a day.

❖ William Shakespeare's real full name was Guilelmus filius Johannes Shakespere. And the name of William was given by his godfather William Smith, a haberdasher. So Shakespeare became like a salesman as his godfather, he sold not needles, pins, cotton and buttons, but the performances of various plays.

❖ Every year has four faces-spring, summer, fall and winter, but every man has three stages – childhood, youth and old age, so that's a proverb - the fathers count up to three.

❖ What is happiness, and how can one lead a happy life? Life is full of joy, sorrow, and grief. Trees are joyful when they have fruit, and sad when a gardener doesn't look after them. If a man gains a good name during his lifetime he will lead the second life after death. So happiness is like a prince, or princess with good health, wealth, fame and name.

❖ We adore the language of the heart, when it tells us what our head thinks about.

❖ Literature becomes marvelous when the nation and its writers are marvelous.

❖ Stanzas in poetry are the tears of great poets.

❖ My five year old granddaughter Aysu phoned me and said that she would talk to me in the name of my mother. I was embarrassed because my mother died some five or six months ago. But my granddaughter insisted on my listening to the old voice that she imitated:

–It's me, Granny, it's your mam. I died, but it is very dark under the ground. I miss my house, you know it is good to live in a light room.

Then she said nothing. But I looked at the light of my apartment, it seemed to me, my mam was very delighted with that light and on that day she was talking to me all night.

❖ One word is an orphan, two words - a big fun.

❖ Children speak simple words, but adults mostly don't understand each other.

❖ A candle is like a needle; it sews the white shirt for the night.

❖ To become a celebrity is not so easy, it is equal to constructing a city on the sea.

❖ Winds are like freelance writers; they 'write' what they want - and wonder without homage.

❖ Baku is a windy city like Chicago. When there is a traffic jam, just the wind blows, but not cars.

❖ Jalal ad-Din Rumi Movlana wrote in Persian though he was Turkish. And Thomas More was not Roman, and he wrote his 'Utopia' in Latin. So not the writing, but the soul defines the spirit and nationality of the poets.

❖ A book is like a house. The author is the owner, the characters are the author's slaves.

❖ Mostly the people think: how to live to be a hundred, and English think about ninety nine; it is good to keep one year in the mind, because before a child is born, he lives about a year (9 months) in his mother's body.

❖ Read your books while the days are light; or it will be very dark when you die.

❖ You can find the lamb, ham and fish in human flesh; at any time the animal senses will keep the human being alive.

❖ The latest news and sensation have been accepted as the true nature of the nation.

❖ In the world there is a seat of wisdom and they appear not every hour, but very seldom.

❖ If I dare speak about it, that is spirit. Our physical substance is on the Earth, but our Spirit makes its homage in the sky. Our spirit is so tremendous that it flies on the point of our thoughts and fills the infinite sky and lives our eternal life.

❖ Fools create true words, and wise men collect them for the print. That's why they are wise.

❖ Attila was a Hun emperor. His deeds made him famous, but not his name.

❖ If a lady meets her husband with a smile, the life of couples might be a length of million miles.

❖ He who loves his Ophelia will never meet a failure.

❖ One woman in a house is like the Sun, two are a big scandal and a fun, but three will shoot you with a gun.

❖ The wind and the Sun, the rain and snow take the days by their hands and flow like the waters out of river.

❖ Love is as a marvelous marble, death destroys love. It is acting as a black devil.

❖ Sensibility is the best companion of love.

❖ Passion is riding on a horse, when the horse groom is out.

❖ Heart is a hard thing.

❖ Writing is a memorable trace. If it inspires the man's heart, we might say it is smart.

❖ One step is a symbol of risk, the second one is walking tradition.

❖ The drops of the rain are of the same size, they are rhyming like the stanzas by the thunder.

❖ An ant has an extravagant life with his wife and children after the hard labor in winter.

❖ In thesis defence, an applicant had a huge fence, she defended not her ideas, but herself.

❖ We are spiritual existence, and we will exist forever. The drops of river also change - they either give a life to us, or turn into something. So we have various rituals.

❖ A Turkish carpet is designed for an honest man, it usually brings happiness.

❖ They say that the Venetian archives are very famous around the world. So archives are an important source not for writing the scientific history of the world, but the history of archives as well.

❖ One dies of age, the other dies of hatred and revenge, the third dies of hunger, and sometimes of grief and anger. So death brings peace.

❖ Where are you looking to find death? It is in poor and wealthy bodies - it is an invisible clown, which never wears the crown.

❖ Wealth is in soil, water, and in air. Men waste their health for the sake of wealth. And wealth makes people happy, and then it kills men for not sharing it in the right proportion.

❖ The world doesn't have a border, it is infinite, but various countries and nations are shared and divided into lots of cantons. Only God sent its cautions: to live in peace. If you are bothered, there is no use of borders - live as a true man.

❖ On the agenda there was one question: the problem of gender.

❖ Thomas More was a member of the British Parliament. He spoke against Henry VIII much more, at last he was beheaded. Watch yourself, man, never speak more than usual.

❖ Why count chickens in autumn? Better count pence.

❖ If we built our houses in the shape of a circus we would have much more headaches. Better construct a square house with some windows and the door, so we could get out of it, when there is a need.

❖ Once the manuscripts were lost, printed books sold best. Now electronic or screen books are coming forward.

❖ Not the world is the theatre, but the new technology is.

❖ e-mail looks like a male, if you find f-male, I will accept it as a female.

❖ A bird is sleeping on its one leg. It reminds us of a ballerina.

❖ A man is a monster, but a woman is the morning star.

❖ News, news, news,
   N-means nothing
   E-is Europe
   W-is wonders
   S-is seeing.

❖ America is a tremendous echo
   Of the storms of the ocean.
   You find whenever you go
   Success and promotion.

❖ The best word of praise is life, but the worst words is paradise.

❖ They say: history begins in Sumer, the ancient land of Mesopotamia, it became the cradle of the world civilization on the globe between 3500 and 3200 B.C. The invention of writing or creating the first pictorial writing later on turned into words. If I had to change the alphabet, I would prefer just pictorial writing so we could economize words, and speak less.

❖ Writing is a very good practice for better understanding your inner world. But if you plagiarize the ideas, or thoughts of others never turn your wrist, you might get an honor of being the real plagiarist.

❖ Two and two is four. When animals learned arithmetic they started walking on their four legs.

❖ Every animal is beautiful, and we don't take care of it, our goal is to hunt and eat.

❖ Ideas are the property of a writer.

❖ Music has one language, that needs no interpretation.

- Under the tune of charming music we can collect the stars and bring them down.

- Lies are walking in the image of truth. And truth is covered with snow until the rain starts.

- A life after death is a question from the ancient times. But up to date a life lives a maximum 99 years. And we keep one year as a keepsake.

- Trees are like soldiers.

- Light and truth stand shoulder to shoulder, they fight for humans' right, and never die.

- Blind people are fighting for the light, whose clothing is black like the night.

- Goodness and badness are competing to win a competition. But there is a faith that one day goodness will be the winner.

- They say that the Greeks didn't allow women to play in the theatre, and if they were allowed to play in it, the theatres wouldn't survive up to modern times.

- My first ode which I tried to write was a national, or cultural code.

- There is the law of attraction, but this is not an auction, but it is your love's reaction.

- We are not chasing the secret to death, but to life, because the real and better life looks like a sharp knife.

- Never think that life is love to your wife, but it is love to pride.

- Writing everyday a page, seems to me as a joy of an age.

- Sweet wind is a hint of love.

- The world is full of words, we are creators of ideas.

- Modern technology is the voice and the choice of our senses.

- It is not hard to talk to a heart.

- ❖ Through all his life a man leads two lives: he is a lively in the day time, but at night he behaves on a bed - as if he is dead.

- ❖ University delivers two degrees - one is Bachelor's, the other is Master's. But physicians offer the thermometer of Celsi, the other is Fahrenheit.

- ❖ A noble writer rejected the nomination of a Nobel Prize, he was willing to make one letter change in Nobel, 'e' should be after 'l'. In case that will be suitable for him as Noble Prize laureate.

- ❖ Love is abstract, death is reality.

- ❖ When dance is perfect, we say her heart is dancing. But when eloquent speech is heard, we say he is a man of head.

- ❖ What is to think; it is a great chance of imagination - to find something useful.

- ❖ Love is changeable like the wind.

❖ A black crow was crowned when it started to snow. It was sitting on the snow like a black prince.

❖ A day and a night never argue: they share just one clock. After 12 hours the one takes the other's place without a space.

❖ Light confessed its love to the night, it made the night tender and bright. The night was delighted of such a love.

❖ Three apples fell from the heaven. If you eat one you might be sent as Eva to hell. The heaven sends three apples for a judgment when the fairy tale is over.

❖ The first thing is to think about the thing that you know nothing about.

❖ If you have the same blood group with your wife, you will be a good actor of your life.

❖ 'Hamlet - the Prince of Denmark' made Shakespeare very famous as the prince of the plays of England.

❖ My distant relative in the village of Danabash has a beloved ass. That ass never plays in the mud, but takes care of herself with the mirror and my relative gave her the name 'my dear lass'. Is it good or a loss, but the ass after praise behaves not like as a lass, but as an ass.

❖ If you poison the environment, you will not cure it with an ointment. If there is a rain, you will have a pain. Better use your brain.

❖ If you catch a cold, you won't need air conditioning.

❖ Men have the senses of wild animals because they usually eat the wilds.

❖ When the ants have weddings, for flying for a second, they wear their wings. After the weddings the ant groom leads his bride into the underground room.

❖ Word and sword are like twins, but mostly word wins if the sword is dull.

❖ True, or not true, some of my long-legged are friends like a kangaroo.

❖ Love, and death depend on wealth.

❖ Love, and death find relaxation on bed.

❖ To be, or not to be? That is the question of English grammar.

❖ If I were a bee, I would exchange my name with 'to be'.

❖ English Grammar has four tenses. But my grandma' knows just the three. I might die next year? She might not know the 4th tense then.

❖ You are the resident of your country, but your president has in addition a letter 'p' at the beginning of the word, so he is a privileged person.

❖ Dear student, do you know George Bernard Shaw wrote: Better late, than never. But the teachers always say: Never late. My point of view is: Students early, teachers late.

❖ In the dawn the dews on the grasses are like the tears. They are much afraid of being cut down.

❖ *Mr. Falcon, Mr. Falcon,*
Don't you know what you can?
I'm waiting for the birds,
We're singing just the words.

❖ If Nizami Ganjavi were born in America, his world fame might be known overseas. But Azerbaijan is so small and surrounded by the Caspian Sea, nobody sees and recites his majestic treasure of words.

❖ *One, two, three...*
Climb the tree
Counting's over
Number's free.

❖ Words are playing like the running waters in the house.

❖ It is not snowing on the hair, when the sorrow and grief are brushing them with their white colour.

❖ If my literary culture sounds in English, we might be sad, but English might get powerful.

❖ There always has been the generation gap - misunderstanding between a father and a son. What about a father and a daughter? It is not a gap, but a breakdown.

❖ A man in a grave is never brave.

❖ A married woman is willing to be the queen, but she usually gets a title - the spouse.

❖ *No nights,*
No days.
How is coming
Other days.

Three hundred
Sixty five.
Are completely
Mothers' days.

❖ God created the earth, and men invented money and purse.

❖ A poor man has a pure love.

❖ Falling in love is like falling into a manhole.

❖ Love - how do I love you, how can I prove my love if I couldn't find it.

❖ Everybody thinks of great jobs that could bring good money, but great jobs are not for everyone.

❖ 'A night' was very proud that by adding the letter 'k', it could easily become 'a knight'.

❖ Name is good, surname is better, but no name is the best.

❖ If you have nothing to write, you can think all day and night.

❖ Manuscript was the first, book became the second, internet book claimed to be the next. Soil and heaven were very excited, how beautiful it was, when the peasants were cultivating just the soil under the light of the sun.

❖ In autumn the leaves from trees fell down on the ground. Some of them are in the shape of heart, but some are in the shape of hands. I was thinking that when trees fade they embrace the soil with heart and hands.

❖ 26 letters of English are leading the words like generals, but its 44 sounds are making tunes for marching them in the right order.

❖ The soldiers are dreaming to be the generals. But the generals are calmed down, because they will not be soldiers again.

❖ A bird is making one nest to sleep at night, though a man thinks that he is very honest, and builds two or more houses - one in the East, the other in the West.

❖ As long as you live, you will lead it with belief. If you lose your belief, there wouldn't be any relief.

❖ Words are like birds; words are never looking for rest, but birds know where their nest are.

❖ Words and swords are very similar to each other and they are competing, fighting, killing - nobody can predict, whenever one of them will be winner again.

❖ We play with words like toys; toys make the noise and the noise has no choice who to go after.

❖ If I had a chance to talk to William Wordsworth - I would say his Words worth for everything in the universe.

❖ Smoking is a bad habit, but smoke is like transference of words when you choke of grief and search for lost belief.

❖ Speak to me I would tell you who you are.

❖ When a word appeared, it embraced someone calling it the 'world'. So 'L' in that word means just love for it.

❖ Men's best production is the word. The worst is when the bad word becomes the first.

❖ A false man never becomes a true man.

❖ Shakespeare was never against plagiarism, and he wrote his plays just for the sake of rhyme and rhythm.

❖ If you are furious with bureaucracy, and who is curious with democracy.

❖ It is said that the property belongs to God: then why do we have to pay taxes to money collectors.

❖ We know that sheep never go to school; but the shepherds behave like teachers with a big stick in their hands.

❖ The clock is like a hypocritical man: it shows just twelve hours on its one face - but hides its twelve hours on the other one.

❖ Love is blind - I will buy a four-eyed Mercedes to lead my life on.

❖ Widow by accident broke the door and now is going in and out only through the window.

❖ Which is stronger: Love or money? - Fifty-fifty.

❖ When I was a child at the age of six, I was acting like the president in my dreams. But now I am over sixty and willing to send a message for retirement.

❖ Seven days of the weak and seven hills of heaven - don't like the numbers after seven.

❖ Love is a comedy, but death is a tragedy. When love is over, death is stopping to get the power.

❖ Love is stronger than death: when love is bright, death is dying at night.

❖ If a book is a treasure, how do you measure it for your leisure?

❖ A child at home never makes a way to Rome.

❖ Adults acting like a child is a great pleasure for children. Children acting like adults sounds as a strange insult.

❖ Words become dangerous if you put too much salt in it.

❖ The monkey was dreaming not of buying a horse, but just a black donkey, as the last syllable of a word was linked and locked with the key.

❖ Men have two legs, but animals have 4. And if trees could get 2 legs, they might.

❖ I am running after valuable ideas, if I get one, I feel that Columbus discovered the new America.

❖ Time shouldn't be measured by a clock or a watch. Its best measurement is the Sun and the Moon.

❖ If men were born with 4 feet, they wouldn't grow long beard, not to be ashamed of animals. They might think how to hide their back, so there would be a lack of a normal tail.

❖ Sumerian-akkadian, Greek, Latin, Arabian, Ottoman, German, French, then… English became the cultural and world languages. One language can't rule through all ages. So languages compete, there is a feast for powerful carrier of a language, that wins, or becomes the first.

❖ A selfish one doesn't catch, or sell fish, but simply might wish to get a salmon.

❖ Key letters of a word 'sky are 's', 'k' and 'y' that might mean the saint keeper of the yearning.

❖ In Azerbaijan there is a fire place of ever burning gas - its name is Burning Mountain. But a Scottish poet got a similar name, his good poems brought him fame. His name is Robert Burns.

❖ Love and prove were nice rhyme in British Renaissance time. I wouldn't mime it, but the best is love and dove.

❖ You would go too far, said my mom. How could I, if I haven't got a car.

❖ If English were angels, who were devils then…

❖ A man married to a very obedient woman, first he liked calling her 'my rabbit'. After five years she turned from a rabbit into a robot.

❖ Latins had 'AD' and 'BC' calling the two different eras. And English had the same misuse, - the foolish man said. -Better call it in an alphabetical order: 'AB', and then 'CD'. Is it all right, belatedly thought the man.

❖ The poets write in a very chaotic way, sometimes it seems to you it is meaningless. But then you think that you are in a postmodern era.

❖ No pence, no fence.

❖ Poetry is delight and the light. And prose is not a rose that you can throw.

❖ Life and death have been living through eternity - they change their seats every hundred years.

❖ If a man does his duty, fruit of the earth will just be beauty.

❖ A mad man always tells the truth, so that's why he is truly mad.

❖ Imagination is the child of a nation.

❖ To dare means you could be not the worst, but the first.

❖ When beauty is full, it becomes beautiful.

- If you are willing something to buy, get a visa and go to Dubai.

- A passion is like a mode of fashion.

- An honor is not gained in one hour.

- A man of practice is like an actor, or actress.

- A pen and a paper prescribe an ointment which makes something for readers' enjoyment.

- Money is the enemy of honor.

- Understanding of Baku is not just to taste its delicious barbecue, but to know really its name from Arabic 'badi kiba' that means 'the windy city'.

- How to live to be 100? But some men mostly like counting 100 dollars.

- Never ask a lady 'How old are you?' Better say 'How young you are!'

- Better be deaf and dumb than a Parliament speaker.

❖ Harms and charms are rhyming, and competing; they both have arms, but charms try to be the first in the earth.

❖ On the 23rd of April in 1964 there was Shakespeare's birthday commemoration, but on that day an expert of the poet's dramas couldn't attend the meeting, and he sent just a message: 'Happy birthday, Mr. Shakespeare!'

❖ A postman had a long complaint about the millennium that it was not so fair to him. However he was one of the first men who traditionally got the position with the word 'post', now he is expelled from his honorable job, post modernism didn't like his first antagonist.

❖ My friend is a writer who publishes dozen of books every year. He is writing nonsense, the price of the books is not 99 pence, but very, very expensive. The readers buy them not for their content, but for the nice binding and the impressive sounding title.

❖ Oh love, how do I love you. I'm crazy about you: L - is my 'lord'; o - is 'exclamation'; v - is 'very'; and e - is 'eternal'. And I'm intending to join my love on the wings of spirit.

❖ How much are the two verbs alike: one is 'adore', the other is 'abhor'. But the two couldn't live together like Hamlet and Ophelia.

❖ Music is rhythm and inner sound of the heart, it has invisible beauty, it captures the hearts of both fools and wise men.

❖ The word *life* is of four letters and its meaning is life isn't forever.

❖ Love is also of four letters; o my lord, is it a visual embracement?!

❖ A day and a night look like a pair of white and black horses. They are carrying the time of the universe behind them.

❖ They say that Venice was the first centre of opera in Europe, and the first public opera house in the world was constructed in Venice. So opera with its amusing arias won not the souls of people of various areas, but it was transference of a storm of waters into the realm of hearts.

❖ We have love to our past, present and future. But future in the past is a deal of clergy, that is like the fourth microphone of journalism.

❖ People all over the world are working for money like a devil, it can lead man to death.

❖ History is mixed with false and truth.

❖ Every region has its sacred religion, but on the top the highest bust is for God, the creator of earth, and universe.

❖ Iron is looking with irony to Gold, as it was behaving like God in the world of metals.

❖ Some people think that life is a long poem, but in reality life consists of four letters.

❖ We are chasing the best solution of the thoughts like the king.

❖ The truth and the lie are playing the game of cat and mouse. The cat is like the truth, the proof of its fighting is the mouse that is behaving with the food very badly in the house.

❖ Birth, death and earth are like a triangle, but the former two will always compete as long as the universe exists.

❖ If you possess the realm of wisdom it means you are quite old to think about the world.

❖ The mist looks like the spirit of the earth, and the real poem is like the breath of the universe.

❖ The city of Baku is a musical hall when the wind blows; the musician is the wind but it never shows its face.

❖ Wisdom is clothed with words of its own like the mountain with snow.

❖ If students ask teachers more questions, then teachers will have misfortunes.

❖ Life doesn't mean to be a husband and a wife, but it is like a game of a fork and a knife.

- The stream of people is like the stream of water. People rush for money and comfort, but waters intend to make friends with thirsty hearts.

- When Love is lessening, a lover doesn't think about the flower.

- My princess is happiness, and if you are penniless, there is no use crying after pineapples.

- Once we were fire worshippers and still we adore fire and fair ladies.

- A book is like a water-melon, you cannot tell its taste, if you haven't acquainted with thought in it.

- Thoughts are as fruits. But few of them might engage our interest, or taste. Never haste to find a taste.

- Beautiful girls on the street are nicer than flowers in a garden.

❖ A beggar is dreaming to become a president, but the president is willing to go too far, just to become the God.

❖ He who loves not love will debate with hate.

❖ Spring is childhood, summer is youth, autumn is manhood, but winter is the prettiest mood of nature.

❖ If you can compose a definition of love, a dove will sit on your shoulder.

❖ A sonnet is the best way of expression of love with a rhyme, and prime.

❖ The day is over, it is not so far, but still we have some time to be a philosopher.

❖ Discipline your child as a teenager, so you will get the respect that you desire.

Index

Azerbaijan. Officially the Republic of Azerbaijan, the largest country in the Caucasus region located at the crossroads of Western Asia and Eastern Europe *13, 18, 32, 52, 62, 67, 86, 94*

'Being and Nothingness'. Essay on Phenomenological Ontology by Jean-Paul Sartre *26*

Baku. Capital city of the Republic of Azerbaijan. It became important after an earthquake destroyed Shamakhy in the 12th century, when the 12th ruler of the Shirvanshahs Akhsitan I, chose Baku as the new capital *19, 67, 73, 96, 100*

Bakuvite. The citizen of Baku city in the Republic of Azerbaijan *18, 52*

Barrie, Sir J.M. (James Matthew) (1860-1937). Novelist and playwright, born in Kirriemuir, Scotland, educated at Glasgow Academy, Dumfries Academy, and Edinburgh University *41*

Beckett, Samuel (1906-1989). Irish writer, born at Foxrock, Dublin; awarded the Nobel Prize in 1969 *18*

Bellini Gentile (c.1429-February 23, 1507). From 1474 he was the official Italian painter. Artist for the Doges of Venice *45, 57*

Belloc, Hilaire (1870-1953). Poet, critic, historian, novelist, travel writer, and Catholic apologist, born in France but educated at J.H.Newman's Oratory School in Birmingham and at Balliol College, Oxford *46*

Bellow, Saul (1915-2005). American novelist, born in Canada of Russian-Jewish parents *16*

Beowulf. Old English poem of 3,182 lines, surviving in about the years of 1010 *65*

Black Sea, The. Sea in southeastern Europe. It's bounded by Europe Anatolia and the Caucasus, and is ultimately connected to the Atlantic Ocean via the Mediterranean and the Aegean Seas and various straits *11*

Blake, William (1757-1827). Engraver and visionary poet; was a student at the Royal Academy *42*

Borrow, George Henry (1803-1881). British writer, educated in Edinburgh High School and at Norwich *28*

Brute of Troy. Is a legendary descendant of the Trojan hero Aeneas, known in Medieval British legend as the eponymous founder and first king of Britain *60*

Burns, Robert (1759-1796). Scottish poet, born near Alloway in Ayrshire *25, 39, 40, 94*

Byron, George Gordon, sixth Baron (1788-1824). British poet, born in London *24, 33, 42*

Caedmon. (fl.670). Old English poet, the only poem attributed to him is the short 'Hymn of Creation' *57*

Caesar, Gaius Julius (100-44 BC). Roman politician, and a general of genius *55*

Caffa. (Feodosia) (Feodosiya). Port and resort city in Crimea, the Ukraine, on the Black Sea coast. During much of its history the town was known as Caffa or Kaffa *11*

Carpaccio (the paintings). Dish of raw meat or fish, thinly sliced or pounded thin. *45*

Carrol, Lewis (pseudonym of Charles Lutwidge Dodgson) (1832-1898). Celebrated English children's writer, his most famous work was 'Alice's Adventures in Wonderland' (1865) *34*

Caspian Sea, The. The largest enclosed inland body of water on the Earth by area variously classed as the world's largest lake or a full-fledged sea. It is bounded to the northwest by Russia, to the west by Azerbaijan, to the south by Iran, to the southeast by Turkmanistan, and to the northeast by Kazakhstan *38, 86*

Caucasian Albania. Name for the historical region of the eastern Caucasus, existed on the territory of present-day Republic of Azerbaijan and partially southern Daghestan *61*

Caucasus, The. The Region at the border of Europe and Asia, situated between the Black and the Caspian Seas. It is home to the Caucasus Mountains, Europe's highest mountain, Mount Elbrus *24, 61, 62*

Caxton, William (1415/24-1492). Merchant and the first English printer, born in Kent *68*

Chekhov, Anton Pavlovich (1860-1904). Russian dramatist and short story writer, born in Taganrog, and was a medical student in Moscow (1879-1884) *41*

Chicago. Famous as the Windy City in the US *67, 73*

Clare, John (1793-1864). English poet, is recognized as a poet of truth. Born in Helpstone, Northamptonshire. His first book of poetry brought him a tremendous fame. But he spent the end of his life in Asylum as he had mental troubles. While he was in Asylum he declared that 'I was Byron and Shakespeare formerly. At different times … I'm different persons' *10*

Clay, Henry (1777-1852). American lawyer, politician and skilled orator *27*

Coleridge, Samuel Taylor (1772-1834). English poet literary critic and philosopher, was born Devonshire England *20*

Columbus. (1451-1506). Italian explorer, navigator, and colonizer, born in the Republic of Genoa (Italy). He completed 4 voyages across the Atlantic Ocean *93*

Constantinople. The capital of the Roman, Byzantine, Latin and the Ottoman empires *45*

Cummings, E.E. (Edward Estlin) (1894-1962). American poet, born in Cambridge, Massachusetts *16*

Danabash village. Story by Jalil Mammadguluzadeh, Azerbaijani writer and dramatist (1866-1932) *84*

Davies, W.H. (William Henry) (1871-1940). Poet and autobiographer, born in Newport, Monmouthshire, Wales. He went to America, where he spent several years and lost his leg in an accident. His best known poem is 'Leisure' which brought him world-wide fame *17*

Day, John (c.1574-c.1640). Playwright, expelled after a few months from Gonville and Caius College, Cambridge, in 1592 for stealing a book *13*

Dickens, Charles (1812-1870). English novelist, born in Portsmouth, the son of a clerk in the navy pay office *28, 57*

Dickinson, Emily (1830-1886). American poet, born in Amherst, Massachusetts, the daughter of a successful lawyer *36*

Druidism. Ancient religion. For many people in North America their ancestors trace back to Celtic Druidism *59*

Eliot, George (pseudonym of Mary Ann) (1819-1880). English novelist, poet, born in Chilvers Coton, Warwickshire *34*

Elizabeth I. (1533-1603). Daughter of Henry VIII and Anne Boleyn, and queen of England from 1558 up to 1603 *37, 46, 57, 69*

Emerson, Ralph Waldo (1803-1882). American philosopher and poet, born in Boston *28*

Fitzgerald, F. Scott (Francis Scott Key) (1896-1940). American novelist and short story writer, born in Minnesota *17*

Franklin, Benjamin (1706-1790). Political writer and autobiographer, born in Boston *19, 23, 41*

Frost, Robert Lee (1874-1963). American poet, born in San Francisco *25, 40*

Ganjavi, Nizami (1141-1209). Great Azerbaijani poet, born in Ganja, in Azerbaijan *86*

Gazetta (gazette). A news-sheet first published in Venice about the middle of the 16th century *24*

Gilgamesh. The fifth king of Uruk, modern day Iraq. According to the Sumerian King List he reigned for 126 years. In Mesopotamian mythology,

Gilgamesh is a demigod of superhuman strength. He is usually described as two-thirds god and one third man *22*

Globe Theatre. Erected in 1599 *69*

'**Hamlet - the Prince of Denmark**'. A tragedy by William Shakespeare probably written by 1601. Its short text reconstructed from memory by actors was printed in 1603 a complete text in 1604-5 *44*

Hayman, Robert (14 August 1575-November 1629). English poet, colonist and Proprietary Governor of Bristol's Hope colony in Newfoundland. He was born in Wolborough near Newton Abbot *46*

Heine, Heinrich (1797-1856). German poet, born of Jewish parents in Düsseldorf *33*

'**Henry VIII**'. History play generally believed to be a collaboration between William Shakespeare and John Fletcher, based on the life of Henry VIII of England *77*

Henry, O. (pseudonym of William Sydney Porter)(1862-1910). American short story writer, born in North Carolina *34*

Heywood, John (1497-1580). English writer, and playwright *27*

Homer. (supposedly 8th century BC). Poet, or singer of the two great epic poems, the 'Iliad' and the 'Odyssey' of Greek Literature *22, 25, 42*

Hughes, Langston (1902-1967). African American writer, born in Joplin, Missouri, who lived in Harlem after 1947. Leading figure of the Harlem Renaissance *11*

Hughes, Ted (1930-1998). English poet and children's writer, born in Mytholmroyd, in the West Riding district of Yorkshire *12*

Hugo, Victor-Marie (1802-1885). French poet, novelist, the leading figure of the Romantic movement in France *42*

Huns. Nomadic people or peoples, who are known to have lived in Eastern Europe, the Caucasus and Central Asia between the 1st Century AD and the 7th Century *104*

Jerome, Jerome K. (Klapka) (1859-1927). English novelist, dramatist, and journalist, born in Walsall, Staffordshire *28*

Joyce, James (Augustine Aloysius) (1882-1941). Irish writer, born at West Rathgar, Dublin and educated at the Jesuit boarding school, then at the Royal University of Ireland *21, 22, 25, 39*

Keats, John (1795-1821). One of the principal figures in the Romantic movement. Poet, educated at Clarke's school, Enfield *21, 27*

Kafka, Franz (1883-1924). Born in Prague. He was a German-language writer of novels and short stories, regarded by critics as one of the most influential authors of the 20th century. Kafka strongly influenced genres such as existentialism *26*

Lenin, Vladimir Ilyich (Ulyanov) (1870-1924). Russian communist revolutionary, politician, political theorist, the leader of the Russian SSR from 1917, then Premier of the Soviet Union from 1922 until his death; born in Simbirsk, Russia *35*

Limericks. Short humorous, often ribald or nonsense poem, especially one in five line anapestic meter with a strict rhyme scheme (AABBA), which is sometimes obscene with humorous intent *18*

Lincoln, Abraham (1809-1865). The 16th President of the US (1861-1865), born in Hodgenville, Kentucky, USA *11*

Longfellow, Henry Wadsworth (1807-1882). American poet, born in Maine and educated at Bowdoin College *35*

Marcus, Aurelius Antoninus (121 AD-80). Roman emperor 161-80 and stoic philosopher, was the author of 12 books of 'Meditations' *36*

Marquez, Gabriel Garcia (b.1927). Colombian novelist, short story writer, screenwriter, journalist, Nobel Prize winner (1982), born in Aracataca, Colombia *25*

Maugham, William Somerset (1874-1965). English writer and playwright, born in Paris and educated at King's School, Canterbury, and in Heidelberg. He was the author over 30 plays, and lots of short stories *35*

'Merchant of Venice, The'. A comedy by William Shakespeare written in 1596/7 and was printed in 1600 *43, 45*

Mesopotamia. 'Between rivers' is a name for the area of the Tigris-Euphrates river system corresponding to modern day Iraq, Kuwait, the northeastern section of Syria and to a much lesser extent southeastern Turkey and smaller parts of south West Iran *50, 79*

Milton, John (1608-1674). Poet, born in Bread Street, Cheapside. He wrote mostly in Latin *35*

More, Thomas (1478-1535). English lawyer, social philosopher, author, statesman and noted Renaissance humanist. He was an important councilor to Henry VII and Lord Chancellor from 1529 to 1532 *73, 77*

Movlana, Jalal ad-Din Muhammad Rumi (1207-1273). Turkish Sufi poet, well-known for his '*Masnavi-i Manawi*' ('Spiritual Couplets'), born, in Afghanistan *73*

Nabokov, Vladimir Vladimirovich (1899-1977). Russian-born novelist, poet, and literary scholar. He was the son of a leading member of the Cadet party, and of the Kerensky government in Russia. He studied at Cambridge University. For a while lived in Berlin, Paris, in the USA, and Switzerland *26*

Newton, Sir Isaac (1642-1727). Scientist, born in Woolsthorpe, near Grantham, studied in Trinity College Cambridge University *9*

Nobel, Alfred Bernhard (1833-1896). A Swedish chemist distinguished in the development of explosives *58, 82*

Noel, Saint Nicholas. Father Christmas, Kris Kringli and Simply Santa, a mythical figure with legendary, historical and folkloric origins *46, 47*

'Odyssey'. An epic poem traditionally ascribed to Homer *22*

Ophelia. Fictional character in the play 'Hamlet' by W. Shakespeare. She is a young noblewoman of Denmark, the daughter of Polonius, sister of Laertes, and potential wife of Prince Hamlet *74, 98*

Othello. Written in 1603 by W.Shakespeare. Othello, a Moorish general in the Venetian army *45*

Ovid. (Publius Ovidius Naso) (43 BC-17 AD). Latin poet, born at Sulmo (now Sulmona, in Italy), studied oratory in Rome, and visited Athens and other places in the Greek East *21*

Paine, Thomas (1737-1809). Revolutionary and author of pamphlets *31*

Plath, Sylvia (1932-1963). American poet, novelist and short story writer. Born in Boston, is best known for her 2 published collections, 'The colossus and Other Poems' and 'Ariel' *12*

Poe, Edgar Allan (1809-1849). American writer, born in Boston *24*

Pope, Alexander (1688-1744). Poet, son of a Roman Catholic linen draper of London *9*

Reilly O', J.B. (1870-1928). Irish-born poet, journalist and fiction writer. He was a member of the Irish Republican Brotherhood, or Fenians for which he was transported to Western Australia *43*

Renaissance, Harlem. The flourishing of African-American culture and literature. Its centre was Harlem-district of New York *11*

River Ouse. River in North Yorkshire, England. The length is about 84 km, the 6th longest river in the UK *26*

Romanticism. Or Romantic period. Artistic, literary, and intellectual movement towards the end of the XVIII century in Europe *20, 21*

Rowley, William (c.1585-1626). Dramatist and actor. His first compositions were plays for Queen Anne's Men *13*

Ruskin, John (1819-1900). Critic, born in London. He wrote for the Arundel Society, and taught at the Working Men's College. He became the first Slade professor of art at Oxford *23*

Sartre, Jean-Paul (1905-1908). Born in Paris. He was a French philosopher, playwright, novelist, screenwriter, political activist, biographer, and literary critic *26*

Scott, Sir Walter (1771-1832). Scottish novelist, born in College Wynd, Edinburgh *58*

Scythia. A multinational region of Central Eurasia in the classical era, encompassing parts of Pontic steppe, Central Asia, Eastern Europe *38*

Shakespeare, William (second name of Guilelmus filius Johannis Shakespere) (1564-1616). English dramatist, actor, man of the theatre, and poet, born in Stratford-upon-Avon *14, 15, 21, 23, 30, 32, 43, 44, 45, 46, 57, 68, 69, 70, 83, 90, 97*

Shaki. Until 1968 Nukha was a city in Northwestern Azerbaijan. Shaki is situated on the southern part of the Greater Caucasus mountaineous range. The name of the town goes back to the ethnonym of the Sakas, who reached the territory of modern day Azerbaijan in the 7th century BC *19*

Shaw, George Bernard (1856-1950). Irish dramatist and critic, born in Dublin, awarded the Nobel Prize in 1925 *30, 85*

Shelley, Percy Bysshe (1792-1822). English poet and radical, born at Field Place, Sussex *10, 14, 21, 29*

Sidney, Sir Philip (1554-1586). English writer and courtier, born in Penshurst Place, in Kent *37*

Socrates. (469-399 BC). Greek philosopher *23*

Spenser, Edmund (?1552-1599). English poet, probably born in Smithfield, London *38*

Stevenson, Robert Louis (originally Lewis) (1850-1894). Scottish novelist, essayist, and poet, born in Edinburgh *32, 44*

Sumeria. Sumer was an ancient civilization and historical region in Southern Mesopotamia, modern Iraq *22, 93*

Surrey, Henry Howard (1516/17-1547). Poet, 3rd duke of Norfolk. He was with the army during the war with France (1544-1546), and was a commander of Boulogne *37*

Tennyson, Alfred, first Baron Tennyson (1820-1892). English poet, born Somershy, Lincolnshire *9, 31*

Thackeray, William Makepeace (1811-1863). English writer, born in Calcutta *31*

Thatcher, Margaret (1925-2013). British politician, Prime Minister of the UK (1979-1990), the leader of the Conservative Party (1975-1990), born in Grantham, England. Soviet journalists called her the 'Iron Lady' *57*

Thoreau, Henry David (1817-1862). American author, born in Concord, Massachusetts *29, 31*

Tomiris (Tomyris). Queen who reigned over the Massagetae a pastoral-nomadic Iranian people of Central Asia east of the Caspian Sea, in approximately 530 BC *9*

Trinity. In Christianity the union of Father. Son and Holy Spirit as one God *69*

Troy. City, both factual and legendary, in northwest Anatolia in what is now Turkey, south of the southwest end of the Dardanelles / Hellespont and northwest of Mount Ida *42*

Truman, Harry S. (1884-1972). The 33rd President of the US, born in Missouri *25*

Twain, Mark (pseudonym of Samuel Langhorne Clemens) (1835-1910). American writer, born in Florida, Missouri, of a Virginian family, and brought up in Hannibal, Missouri *29, 32*

'Ulysses'. Novel by James Joyce *21, 22, 25*

USSR, The. Former socialist state on the Eurasian continent that existed between 1922 and 1991, governed as a single-party state by the Communist Party. Its capital was Moscow *51*

Venice. City in Italy *11, 24, 43, 45, 46, 56, 57, 98, 99*

Voyage Out, The. The first novel by Virginia Woolf, published in 1915 by Duccworth, and published in the US in 1920 by Doran *26*

Whitman, Walt (1819-1892). American poet, born on Long Island, New York. He had little education, but his 'Leaves of Grass' (1855) was 'the most extraordinary piece of wit and wisdom that America has yet contributed' (poet and philosopher Ralph Waldo Emerson, 1803-1882 *5*

Wilkins John (1614/19-1672). English clergyman, natural philosopher and author *13*

Woolf, (Adeline) **Virginia** (1882-1941). One of the great innovative English novelists of the XX century, born at Hyde Park Gate *26*

Wordsworth, William (1770-1850). English poet, born at Cockermouth, Cumbria *33, 90*

Wyatt, Sir Thomas (c.1503-1542). Poet, from a Yorkshire family, educated at St. John's College, Cambridge *37*

Yeats, William Butler (1865-1939). Irish poet, dramatist, essayist, autobiographer, and dominating figure of the Irish Revival, born in Dublin *13, 64*

P.S. Auden, Wystan Hugh (1907-1973) British and American poet, writer, critic. He was Professor of Poetry at Oxford University. Married Erika Mann, the daughter of Thomas Mann and emigrated to the USA in 1939 and became an American citizen in 1945. His books of verse and prose brought him reputation as a sharp-edged and witty poet, writer and critic *cover page*